© 2024 Mr Ali. All rights ı

No part of this book may be reproduced, distributed, or transmitted in any form or by any means, including photocopying, recording, or other electronic or mechanical methods, without the prior written permission of the publisher, except in the case of brief quotations embodied in critical reviews and certain other non-commercial uses permitted by copyright law.

No quotes have been directly taken but were deeply thought at the time of teaching based on the situation of the class at the time. It may well be of coincidence and similar context of other quotes.

Every effort has been made to keep the book as simple as possible with the intention of manifesting the quotes daily.

Introduction:

Unlock the power of daily motivation with "Quotivational," a collection of insightful quotes used by a secondary teacher in the United Kingdom. These quotes resonate deeply with students and adults alike. Each quote in this book serves as a daily touchstone, encouraging readers to connect with their hearts and embrace the relentless drive needed to overcome fears and achieve greatness.

For students and adults, "Quotivational" offers a unique opportunity to share these impactful quotes to apply in your lives. By adding personal stories and experiences after reading each quote, adults can demonstrate the real-world application of these timeless lessons, inspiring young minds to strive for success and navigate their own journeys with confidence and resilience.

How to use the book

Transform each day with a quote a day that sparks inspiration, cultivates passion, and sets the stage for a lifetime of achievement. Share the journey, share the success, witness the students soar beyond their dreams and visions. Read one quote and share your own experience to others. Connect deeply with the quote for that day and act upon this. The aim is to finish the book in one year!

The book starts from the beginning of the academic year. Adults can definitely benefit too with an open mind and a calm heart. A few words of encouragement read daily is the essence of success regardless of ability. Some quotes are similar but the growth mind-set needs reminders. Start the book from the month and date you start or wait for September. Hearts will be healed with this soul connecting journey.

Special Thank You

I am forever grateful for my faith and the values it teaches me, as well as my parents, family, and friends who believed in me. I also owe a great deal to my teachers who have helped me achieve greatness and to my colleagues for their support with the vision. Lastly, I want to thank all my amazing students, past and present, who have encouraged me to write this book and who have been aided by many quotes in their moments of perseverance. I am especially grateful to the current secondary students of my Year 8 class at the time of writing this book; they have given me the final courage to write. They have inspired me to fulfil my own dreams! These students were amazing and responded well to advice, especially during exam periods. They believe that this book will help students and adults around the world

September

1. Never allow the fear of failure to outweigh your desire for success. Aim high and stay focused.
2. Always be yourself, but strive to be the best version of yourself.
3. Ensure that today is better than yesterday and that tomorrow will be better than today.
4. The sacrifices you make now to become great are necessary. Embrace them.

5. Your hard work today will make the world a better place tomorrow.

6. The greater the goal, the more planning is required. Prepare meticulously.

7. Even in negative situations, there are lessons to be learned. Seek them out.

8. Never leave anyone behind. True loyalty requires moral values.

9. Believe in yourself. Unleash the greatness within your heart.

10. Speak from the heart so you can connect with others' hearts.

11. Rejections are lessons for greater opportunities. Embrace them as stepping stones.

12. Leave your past behind, only visiting it to appreciate your present.

13. Read books to connect with the world. Knowledge is power.

14. You are in this world to lead people from the darkness of evil into the light of good.

15. Create a team of friends whose hearts are purer than gold.

16. Be the first to try and take risks. Only then will success unravel.

17. Focus on the person you see in the mirror, rather than on others' faults.

18. Never embarrass anyone who is trying to be a better version of themselves.

19. Be calm in difficult moments; ease will follow shortly after.

20. Trust yourself; you can always do better than you are now.

21. Eradicate the obstacles to your success with focus and determination.

22. Take care of the needy. Remember the times you were in need.

23. Count the productive days that have passed. Reflect on your progress.

24. Find solutions to problems. Start with a positive attitude.

25. Humanity is using your gifts to uplift others. Be generous.

26. Even if you live for 1,000 years, you will only leave your legacy behind.

27. The present shapes your future. Focus on the now.

28. Be grateful for what you have; then, more will come.

29. Accept that one day you will leave this world. Let this awaken your soul to change the world.

30. Appreciate everyone in your life. This is the key to good character.

October

1. Endure the short-term pain of early mornings, less socialising, and late nights to avoid long-term pain and failure.

2. Never fear the exam paper; it should fear you!

3. Remember: You will be tested to see how great you are.

4. Repetition is key to creating a cycle of ambitious goals.

5. Money is the reward for all the hard work you do now.

6. Ridiculing the overpowered only hurts yourself more.

7. Respect your elders; only with their experience and wisdom will you find yourself.

8. Be kind and expect nothing in return. That is the definition of real success.

9. Walk and sit firmly; that is when you are ready to face any challenge.

10. Speak little and listen more.

11. Everyone is going through something. Remind them of how great they really are.

12. Time used wisely now means more time in the future when it matters.

13. Complete all tasks immediately after planning.

14. Create a goal that brings people together.

15. Keep yourself away from any matter that affects your vision and disrupts your energy.

16. Believe that you are great. Visualise it.

17. Before you close your eyes and sleep, dream about your goals and achieving them.

18. Do not worry about matters you have no control over.

19. Stop only when the work is done. Take a short rest, then continue pursuing your dream.

20. A true gift is the opportunity to wake up on earth so you can conquer the world through greatness.

21. The road to success must have challenges ahead. Embrace them.

22. Doing the easy work now means harder work later.

23. The present moment is your time to attract greatness. Stop overthinking.

24. A real friend will help you accomplish amazing goals.

25. Serve those in need by working hard now.

26. Success is a lonely journey. Become self-reliant.

27. A perfect life means being the best version of yourself.

28. Plan ahead and keep your next move a secret. Your actions will prove it to all.

29. The roots of a tree that remains upright can withstand any storm.

30. Speak about your world-changing goals to the universe.

31. Be prepared to fail in order to go beyond levels

November

1. A pure mind thinks only what a pure heart feels.

2. Be the one in your family to take success to a whole new level.

3. In life, you will be tested to accomplish true greatness.

4. Persevere through the most difficult trials.

5. Speak only to uplift; otherwise, remain calm and content.

6. In the classroom, be so respectful that your teachers see your desire for greatness.

7. Success has no final destination; it is over time that you will see yourself winning repeatedly.

8. Sometimes you have to be uncomfortable to appreciate true comfort.

9. Even if one person follows your great path, that would suffice.

10. Speak up about your vision. The world's opinions do not matter on your path.

11. Being afraid of failure is the correct mind-set to hold.

12. If you focus on a negative past, your future will be full of negativity.

13. A great life is like solving an equation. Apply the inverse at each step to find the solution.

14. Live as though tomorrow is not guaranteed.

15. Focus your eyes on nature, and you will become a natural at everything.

16. Even on cold nights, your vision should give you warmth.

17. Articulate success through hard work and determination.

18. Trying and failing will lead to prevailing success.

19. Be the first to smile at others, even if your pain doesn't allow you to.

20. Find a mentor who replicates the great leaders of the past.

21. Ahead of you lie opportunities; behind you lie positive moments of growth.

22. Control your tongue; that vessel can cause real pain.

23. Treat every day as though it is your last.

24. The world received an amazing blessing on the day you were born. You are amazing.

25. The pain you are going through in life is to make you, not to break you.

26. The best gift in life is time; it belongs only to you.

27. When the going gets tough, get tougher.

28. We build character in challenging moments.

29. Victory is never achieved alone. Someone believed in you.

30. Sometimes you must let the tears roll, so let them water your soul.

December

1. The cold mornings are overcome by the heat of your dreams. Keep moving forward.
2. The real distraction in life is procrastination. Avoid it.
3. Act upon your positive thoughts in the light of day.
4. Have access to more books than distracting friendships.
5. Ask your heart questions that will unleash the right path.

6. Be happy for others, but first be happy for yourself because that is the fruit of your dedication.

7. Real happiness is remaining positive despite brokenness.

8. In the exam hall, new opportunities open up.

9. The less negative pain your heart possesses, the more you will achieve greatness.

10. Find the love of learning that surpasses earnings.

11. Be at the service of people. By doing this, the world will bring you greatness.

12. Have a vision that sounds unrealistic. Only then will you change the world.

13. Speaking less results in more power through listening more.

14. Aiming for luxury is the first step to misery.

15. Every exam in life will either bring gains or losses.

16. You will be hurt by others. Silence them with your hard work.

17. Contemplate on your journey back home.

18. One day, you will become a champion from the classroom desk to your dream.

19. If life was easy, you would not be needed.

20. Always unconditionally appreciate and hold onto uplifting people.

21. Congratulate yourself for everything you have accomplished so far.

22. Even if everything is against you, believe that you will become great.

23. Empathy is the only way to live a calm life.

24. Always appreciate your neighbour. You may not have a chance to knock again.

25. Bring people together with your positive energy.

26. Be relentless in your tasks; only time will give the result.

27. Ensure every aspect of your life is connected like a beautiful tessellation.

28. Convince yourself that you will leave a legacy for the world.

29. Endure the short-term pain of late nights, early mornings, and studying to avoid the long-term pain of failure and regrets.

30. You are the reason why the world is getting better. Continue to strive.

31. Every moment in your life was predestined to reach something more greater.

January

1. Always believe that change is imminent.
2. Surround yourself with those who have learned from failure.
3. Create such routines that success will happen at all costs.
4. Every individual is going through something. Let them continue their journey.
5. Success is a journey, not a destination.

6. Work so hard in every action that it brings you closer to your goals.

7. Do not fear failure. Fear not trying.

8. Gratitude is the best attitude.

9. Do not chase money. Your hard work and self-belief will bring money to you.

10. Always help those in need, even if nothing is returned to you.

11. You are in the world to make it a better place.

12. The day you were born was a blessing to the world. Persevere.

13. Follow your heart. Sometimes your mind cannot think what your heart believes.

14. You will go through pain and failure. These are learning curves.

15. Today must be better than yesterday, and tomorrow

16. Take daily steps toward your success.

17. Rise early to seize every waking hour.

18. Challenging paths often lead to beautiful destinations.

19. Find a sanctuary to refocus your mind.

20. Write down your goals and dreams. Reflect on them during calm and tough times.

21. Keep your life discreet. Share your dreams with genuine people only.

22. Liberate yourself by mastering your anger and tongue.

23. Discover your purpose through hard work.

24. Face challenges head-on; this is how champions are made.

25. Be kind, even to those who doubt your intentions.

26. Embrace silence as a path to victory.

27. Confidence grows when your vision keeps you awake.

28. Celebrate your accomplishments, knowing there's more to achieve.

29. Transform negative memories into a positive future.

30. Lead the world to greatness despite its trials.

31. Create the best moments in your life with the pain you endure.

February

1. Trust yourself before building trust with others.
2. Never apologise when you're not wrong.
3. Stay calm in difficult moments; success will follow.
4. Someone is always working harder. Don't procrastinate.
5. A caring teacher inspires you to dare.
6. Stay humble to avoid stumbling.

7. When disrespected, respond with success, not retaliation.
8. To find the mean average, sum the numbers and divide by the total count.
9. Success can be lonely; find strength within.
10. Think about your goals, and let them fill your dreams.
11. Avoid distractions and focus on your relentless passion.
12. Stay busy with your dreams, leaving no room for negativity.

13. Help at home; what goes around comes around.
14. Network with your future self for perspective.
15. Forgive before you sleep, and you'll sleep peacefully.
16. Complete tasks promptly to master your time.
17. Call it a character-building day, not a difficult one.
18. Self-belief is crucial in challenging times.
19. The worst betrayal is giving up on your dreams.

20. Visit your past to learn, but don't live there.
21. Taking risks builds strength.
22. Have high expectations, and greatness will follow.
23. Rise higher each time you fall.
24. Don't let adversity define you.
25. A life of struggle is blessed; armour your mind with dreams.
26. Speak with conviction; success is imminent.
27. Purposeful dreams energise you.

28. Protect people from evil,
    don't be suspicious.
29. When one door closes,
    another will open.

March

1. What legacy will you leave? Even a thousand years won't last forever.
2. Each day is a new page in your book; write it well.
3. Competition elevates everyone to the next level.
4. Two negatives make a positive; remember this in tough times.
5. Embrace unexpected opportunities as blessings.

6. Promise those who support you that their struggles will end.
7. Never lose hope; always stay hopeful.
8. Affirm now that your determination will better the world.
9. True power is channelling anger into hard work.
10. Obsession with goals keeps you ahead.
11. If they say enjoy life more, you're on the right path.

12. Each passing day brings you closer to your goal.
13. Life, like a Fibonacci sequence, builds on each previous step.
14. Advocate for justice in this world.
15. Dreams are endless; give them life and meaning.
16. Consistency is key to hard work.
17. Ask yourself why you're here and what you truly aspire to.
18. Finish what you start.

19. Pay the price for success; it's worth every penny.
20. Great days are followed by tests.
21. Emotional intelligence attracts the right people to your dreams.
22. Tears can overcome fears.
23. Light up the darkest night with your plans.
24. Solving equations requires applying the inverse.
25. Pain tests you, but you gain strength from it.

26. Nothing can deter you from greatness.
27. Each defining moment requires a character boost.
28. Guard your heart and mind from negative thoughts.
29. Daily reminders keep you focused.
30. Proactively develop yourself for a brighter future.
31. Every successful leader has overcome unimaginable failures.

April

1. Show empathy to those less fortunate.
2. Be the first to help those in need.
3. Be the first to take action towards greatness.
4. Prove the doubters wrong.
5. Righteous character grants special status.
6. A world-changing vision leads to an exciting life.
7. True freedom is controlling every moment of your life.

8. Completing tasks immediately gives you leverage.
9. Even if the world doubts you, believe in yourself.
10. Be thankful for your infinite blessings before sleep.
11. Travel the world through your studies.
12. Cherish the memories of struggles as you create new ones.
13. Connect to your spiritual self in moments of doubt.

14. Find time to connect with nature.
15. Value the present as you look forward to the future.
16. A believing soul has a high probability of success.
17. Happiness stems from serving those in need.
18. Always remember the teachers who challenged you.
19. Honour those who wish the best for you.
20. Ensure you run the day, not the other way around.

21. Be optimistic about your future self.
22. Mistakes that improve you are lessons learned.
23. Hard work now creates a future of possibilities.
24. Take advice that builds outstanding character.
25. Control your heart with positive thoughts.
26. Evil exists; be the light of good in your dreams.
27. Find and add value with your unique talents.

28. Budget your time and resources for success.
29. Never forget those who helped you reach your dreams.
30. Reach beyond your targets and aims by outstanding practice.

May

1. The toughest tests bring out your best.
2. Your passion will uplift others if it resonates positively.
3. Integrity in hard work attracts followers.
4. Hard tests make you stronger.
5. Aspire to the highest level of noble ambition.
6. Don't fear the exam paper; let it fear you.
7. Work hard now to achieve greatness.

8. Conceal your problems; you will prevail.
9. Show compassion, especially to those who benefit most.
10. Inheriting greatness is more valuable than wealth.
11. Realise your blessings outweigh complaints, and the world is yours.
12. Use your time wisely, especially during exams.
13. Improvement is greater than perfection.

14. Resilience means thriving in uncertainty.
15. Promise yourself to achieve your dreams.
16. Time to accomplish is now; only passion will get you there.
17. Success can be lonely.
18. Difficult roads lead to the right path.
19. Choose wisely and beyond emotions.
20. Birds follow a leader; so should you.

21. Each day brings a new challenge; be ferocious.
22. Tenacity in hard work outshines softness.
23. Suffer not when your dreams are alive.
24. Treat every exam mark as world-changing.
25. Connect deeply with your soul.
26. True power comes from a heart passionate about greatness.

27. Turn your difficult path into a success story.
28. To reach the peak, accept the path.
29. Appreciate each action step towards your dreams.
30. Your future lies ahead; the past is done.
31. You must create your own destiny by the relentless hours of dedication

June

1. A surd, though irrational, has immense value.
2. Inspire others to find their purpose.
3. When a decision is made, be firm.
4. Rectify the past with acts of generosity.
5. Keep your plans private from those with conflicting intentions.
6. Distance yourself from distractions.

7. Your hard work is crafting a future story.
8. Strive for progress, not perfection.
9. Don't be discouraged by what's missing; dreams fill gaps.
10. Worry is natural; find ways to calm your soul.
11. Meditate to soothe restlessness.
12. As an ambassador for greatness, know no limits.

13. Write down moments of appreciation.
14. Accomplish your human duties for the best moments.
15. Believe in your amazing character.
16. Each level up requires a new you.
17. Seize unique, instantaneous opportunities.
18. Speak from the heart but listen with your soul.

19. Value and honour those who help you achieve your dreams.
20. Instead of saying something is wrong, find ways to correct it.
21. Let your facial expressions speak volumes.
22. Develop various skills now even though you may not be rewarded for it.
23. Seek forgiveness by doing good for others.
24. See rain as a blessing.

25. Don't judge those striving to better the world.
26. Work daily towards your dreams without haste.
27. Be grateful for the sacrifices behind your luxuries.
28. Victory hinges on working towards your dreams.
29. Ignore those who haven't faced hardship.
30. Every successful person faced make-or-break moments.

July

1. Seize every opportunity to reach your potential.
2. Unite people for a good cause.
3. With more success, expect trials and tribulations.
4. Welcome your passion; be the last to speak.
5. A vision that creates leaders is the right path.
6. Never undervalue good deeds; encourage others.

7. Be calm and polite but speak out against injustice.
8. Pause before speaking with conviction.
9. Success starts with knowing and believing in yourself.
10. Teachers who challenge you are your dream weavers.
11. Find long-term solutions for short-term discomforts.
12. Give your first earnings to loved ones and those in need.
13. Smooth sailing resembles a direct proportion graph.

14. Different stages of life will test your worth.
15. Surround yourself with great people, not negative ones.
16. You are the average of those around you.
17. Help others without being asked; good will come to you.
18. Inspire others by hiding your struggles on the path to success.
19. Daily reminders are the key to success.

20. Never let absence hinder your ambition.
21. Seek a leader, not just a mentor.
22. Connect emotionally with every conversation.
23. The best days come from achieving your dreams and beyond.
24. Sleep with a forgiving heart, a mind at peace.
25. Expect nothing in return for genuine help.
26. Learn from past failures.

27. Align with people who share your core values.
28. A positive outlook on failure brings greatness.
29. You are what you believe; have faith in opportunities.
30. Imperfections make life purposeful.
31. Create solutions, don't dwell on problems.

August

1. Master one skill rather than knowing many imperfectly.

2. True happiness comes from adding value to those in need.

3. Keep your heart away from dark valleys.

4. Easy tasks often precede challenging ones.

5. Limit over-worrying by focusing on reality and purpose.

6. People will always find ways to distract you. Lead from the front.

7. Give life your vision and dreams. Don't take them to the grave.

8. Disappointments and rejections are the best moments in life.

9. Find a way to let go rather than holding on.

10. The past cannot create your future. Focus on the present.

11. Never wish for life to become easy. Rather, become stronger in mind and heart.

12. Be excited to make the world more advanced.

13. Always be unpredictable around your competitors.

14. Controlled desire brings more contentment.

15. Spend some time alone, sitting on green grass, facing a sea of dreams, and looking up at the limitless sky.

16. Avoid arrogance, as it will destroy your path to greatness.

17. Humility is key to exponential strength.

18. Work so hard that every step leads to further success.

19. Correcting your own faults should be your focus.

20. You can become a winner, but imagine being a champion.

21. Running away from reality will result in facing it more.

22. Always give more of your amazing character than you receive.

23. Keep your good deeds secret and away from display.

24. Never share your deep secrets, even with a close companion.

25. True greatness requires shouldering the burdensome responsibility of fulfilling the rights of the needy.

26. Avoid the spotlight as much as possible. Live a life of attaining success under the radar.

27. These daily special reminders help you stay on a positive path.

28. Create endless possibilities by proving your greatness to the world.

29. There will always be those who create obstacles. Remain strong.

30. What is not meant to be accepted often becomes a blessing later.

31. Have a blessed life through your passion, belief and values.

Be Passionate

Every moment of happiness is desired with MULTIPLICATION.

Explore the truth, find your purpose, keep your ties of kinship without DIVISION.

Take life one step at a time, just like TRANSLATION.

Be humble and firm, and you will see the best view as you have inside and front ELEVATION.

Move along with helping the world so that nobody is left behind, without SUBTRACTION.

See every difficult moment as an EQUATION.

We do the inverse to solve and better the SITUATION.

Life will throw you variables to find together, just like a COMPOSITE FUNCTION.

We need to work together and end sadness with a POSITIVE SOLUTION.

Do not just chase the money; work hard and it will come to you as an ADDITION.

When the going gets tough, think of a LINEAR FUNCTION.
The only way is up, just like a DIRECT PROPORTION.
You are worthy of GREATNESS, just as you solved a SIMULTANEOUS EQUATION.
Always care for the needy, expecting nothing in ROTATION.
Do not be ignorant; it is time for your TRANSFORMATION.
Solve every irrational moment just like a SURD RATIONALISATION.

Keep your life in order, just like BIDMAS OPERATION.

Never give up on your vision, dreams, and ambitions without SUBSTITUTION.

Be confident in your skills; try and simplify, like an ALGEBRAIC EXPRESSION.

Take risks through trials and improvements, just as you did in ITERATION.

Have a plan; don't go sideways and view it like FRONT ELEVATION.

*Simplify situations in your life;
don't blame others but look at
your own REFLECTION.
All your answers are found in the
person you look at in the mirror
without DEPRECIATION.
Expand your empire, as you did in
LOCI and CONSTRUCTION.
Think beyond your area, just as
you drew an inequality REGION.
Have a blessed life. Thank you for
all your hard work and
APPRECIATION.*

Printed in Great Britain
by Amazon